Finches

The Complete Finch Owner's Guide

Including Types, Care, Where to Buy, Temperament, Health, Breeding, Feeding, and Much More!

By Lolly Brown

Foreword

With their bright colors and cheery personalities, finches are some of the most popular pet birds. The name "finch" actually applies to a wide variety of small birds, many of which make great pets. If you are thinking about getting a pet bird, certain species of finch might be good options to consider. Before you go out and buy a finch, however, you should learn as much as you can about them to ensure that it truly is the right pet for you and that you are equipped to care for it properly. You should also learn the difference between the various species so you can choose one that is the right fit.

If you think that a finch might be the right pet for you, this book is the perfect place to start your journey into bird ownership. In this book you will find a wealth of information about finches in general as well as specifics regarding care, feeding, breeding, and more. By the time you finish this book you will not only have a deeper understanding of the finch as a pet, but you will know for sure whether or not it is the right pet for you. If it is, the information in this book will have you well on your way to becoming the best bird owner you can be!

Table of Contents

Chapter One: Introduction

The brightly colored Gouldian Finch is one of the most beautiful finch species while the Zebra Finch makes for a social and entertaining pet. Finches come in all shapes, sizes, and colors which makes them one of the most popular groups of birds to be kept as pets. Although finches are beautiful and unique little birds, they do require a certain degree of care which means that you need to do your research before bringing one home. Not only do you need to learn the basics about finches, but you should also familiarize yourself with the specific requirements of whatever finch species you choose to keep.

In this book you will find a general introduction to finches in general including popular species and basic facts. You will also receive an in-depth look at some of the different finch species, including those that are most popular as pets. In reading this book you will learn everything you need to know in order to make an informed decision regarding whether or not finches are the right pet for you. If you think that they are, you will also receive the practical information you need to prepare your home for your new pets and to take care of them properly.

So, if you are ready to learn more about finches as pets and about finches in general, turn the page and keep reading!

Glossary of Important Terms

Avian – Pertaining to birds.

Axillars – The feathers located on the underside at the base of a bird's wing.

Beak – The mouth of a bird consisting of the upper and lower mandibles.

Breast – The chest of a bird located between the chin and the abdomen.

Brood – The offspring of birds.

Chick – A newly hatched bird; a baby bird.

Cloaca – The aperture through which birds excrete; also the location where eggs and sperm exit the body.

Clutch – The eggs laid by a female bird in a single setting.

Down Feathers – The small feathers that keep a bird warm.

Endemic – Referring to a species that is only found in a particular area.

Fledgling – A young bird that is old enough to leave the nest but still largely depends on the parents.

Flight Feathers – Groups of later feathers found on the wing and tail; includes primary, secondary, and tertiary feathers.

Flock – A group of birds.

Genealogy – The history of the descent of a particular species from its ancestors.

Hatching – The process through which baby birds emerge from the egg.

Hatchling - A newly hatched chick.

Hybrid – The offspring of two different species.

Incubation – The act of resting on eggs to generate heat which causes the eggs to eventually hatch.

Molt – The process through which a bird loses its feathers and grows new ones.

Ornithologist – A professional who studies birds.

Pair Bond – The bond formed between a male and female bird for nesting and breeding purposes.

Pinfeathers – The tiny, developing feathers that emerge from the skin.

Remiges – The wing feathers of a bird.

Retrices – The tail feathers of a bird.

Sexual Dimorphism – Referring to physical differences between the sexes of the same species.

Taxonomy – The classification of species into order, family, genera, etc.

Chapter Two: Understanding Finches

Although you may be familiar with finches in general, there is a lot to learn about these lovely little birds before you decide whether or not they are the right pet for you. Not only are there many different species of finch, but each species has its own unique requirements for care and keeping. In this chapter you will receive an overview of finches in general as well as a detailed description of some of the most popular finch species kept as pets. This information will help you to decide if finches might be a good pet for you and your family.

1.) *What Are Finches?*

The name "finch" is given to a variety of small to medium-sized birds, though not all of them are considered "true finches". The birds known as "true finches" belong to the taxonomical family Fringillidae and they have conical bills, an adaptation for eating seeds, as well as bright and colorful feathers. Finches can be found in a wide variety of different habitats all over the world except in arctic regions and in Australia. Besides the "true finches," other birds that carry the name "finch" belong to various taxonomical families including Estrildidae (known as estrildid finches), Emberizidae (the American sparrow family), and Thraupidae (the tanager family).

Different types of finches can be found in different habitats. For the most part, passerine birds are found in the Northern Hemisphere, but there are some species native to the Neotropic regions of the world. As it has already been mentioned, "true finches" can be found in nearly every part of the world except in Australia and in arctic regions. Estrildid finches, on the other hand, tend to inhabit Australia as well as the Old World tropics. Finches generally live in wooded areas, though some species can be found in deserts or mountainous regions. Some species of finch even have special adaptations that enable them to thrive in their particular habitat.

2.) *Facts About Finches*

Though there are many species that carry the "finch" name, they all belong to the order Passeriformes. This is why finches are sometimes called passerine birds. Within the order Passeriformes there are two main families of finches – the true finches belonging to the family Fringillidae and the waxbills or estrildid finches belonging to the family Estrildidae. There are more than 5,000 species of passerine birds. In fact, nearly half of all the bird species in existence belong to the order Passeriformes.

Finches, as a type of passerine bird, generally have four toes on each of their feet – three of these toes face forward and the fourth faces backward. This particular toe arrangement is called anisodactyl arrangement and it is what enables finches to perch on horizontal surfaces such as branches as well as vertical surfaces like tree trunks. Unlike some birds (mainly waterfowl), finches do not have any webbing between their toes.

Not only are finches unique from other birds due to the anisodactyl arrangement of their toes, but they have another special adaptation that allows them to sleep while perched. Finches have a special tendon that runs down the back of each leg, causing the muscles in the leg to tighten when the leg is bent. When the muscles in the leg tighten, the toes curl and hold their position. This is what happens when a finch lands on a perch and it is also what keeps the bird form falling off its perch even when it is asleep.

While the details vary from one species to another, finches are usually small to medium-sized birds. The smallest of the true finches is the Andean Siskin (*Spinus spinescens*) which stands 3.8 inches (9.5 cm) tall. The largest finch is the Collared Grosbeak (*Mycerobas affinis*) which stands up to 9.4 inches (24 cm) tall and weighs up to 2.9 ounces (83 g). Finches usually have large, strong, and stubby beaks, though there can be a lot of variation in beak size and shape among the different finch species. This is largely due to adaptive radiation – rapid evolutionary changes caused by a change in environment.

When it comes to their plumage, true finches have nine remiges (primary feathers) and twelve rectrices secondary feathers). In most species, the base color is some shade of brown, sometimes with a greenish tint. Many finches have black patches or bars on their feathers, though white plumage is fairly rare except in signaling marks or wing bars. Bright yellow and red colors are also fairly common among various finch species. Many species also exhibit sexual dichromatism with the female of certain species lacking the bright coloring exhibit by the male.

Though each species is unique, many finches have a sort of bouncing flight pattern – they alternate between brief periods of flapping their wings and periods of gliding with their wings closed. Some finch species are very vocal (sometimes to the point of being noisy) and the males of many finch species sing as a means of attracting a mate. When it comes to breeding, finches tend to lay colored eggs and the average clutch size ranges from 3 to 8 eggs, depending on the species. Finch chicks are born featherless and blind so they require a great deal of parental care for the first few weeks but once they are mature enough to fly on their own they are ready to become independent.

Summary of Facts

- **Classification**: order Passeriformes; family Fringillidae, Estrildidae, Emberizidae, or Thraupidae

- **Distribution**: primarily the Northern Hemisphere; true finches are found worldwide except in Australia and arctic regions; estrildid finches are found in Australia and in Old World tropical regions
- **Habitat**: primarily forested areas; some species can be found in the desert or mountainous regions
- **Anatomical Adaptations**: large, stout bills adapted to specific dietary preferences
- **Eggs**: generally 3 to 8 per clutch; 2 to 3 broods per year; eggs are usually colored
- **Incubation Period**: average 13 to 14 days
- **Hatchling**: young birds leave the next after 14 to 21 days, average 15 to 17 days
- **Smallest Size**: Andean Siskin (*Spinus spinescens*) at 3.8 inches (9.5 cm)
- **Largest Size**: Collared Grosbeak (*Mycerobas affinis*) at 9.4 inches (24 cm)
- **Wingspan**: about 8 to 9 inches (20 to 23 cm)
- **Coloration**: wide variety of colors and patterns; base color is usually gray or green; many species exhibit black patches or bars; red and yellow is common
- **Sexual Dimorphism**: male is more brightly colored and tends to sing more
- **Diet**: mostly seeds (granivorous); some species eat berries and small insects

- **Vocalization**: most species vocalize with males of the species singing the most; some species can be very loud and boisterous
- **Lifespan**: average 4 to 7 years

3.) Types of Finches

The Passerine order contains thousands of unique species and the Fringillidae family contains roughly 218 species divided over 52 different genera and 3 different subfamilies. These three subfamilies are Fringillinae, Euphoniinae, and Carduilinae. The Estrildidae family contains a wide variety of small finch species and the Emberizidae family contains several hundred species of buntings, American sparrows, brush-finches, and more. The family Thraupidae, also known as the tanager family, contains the species known as Darwin's finches.

Although there are hundreds of different species of finch, not all of them are popular for keeping as pets. In fact, it is only certain domesticated species of finch that are even legal to keep. Wild species of finch are illegal to keep as pets so, if you are considering finches as pets, make sure you pick a domesticated species and ensure that the bird you purchase is captive-bred, not wild-caught. Some of the most popular species of pet finches include:

- Zebra Finch (*Taeniopygia guttata*)
- Gouldian Finch (*Erythrura gouldiae*)
- Society Finch (*Lonchura striata domestica*)
- Star Finch (*Neochmia ruficauda*)
- Owl Finch (*Taeniopygia bichenovii*)
- Strawberry Finch (*Amandava amandava*)
- Spice Finch (*Lonchura punctulata*)

The species listed above are some of the most popular finch species kept as pets. In the following pages you will receive an introduction to each of these species so you can think about whether or not they might be the right pet for you.

a.) Zebra Finch (Taeniopygia guttata)

The Zebra Finch is by far one of the most popular finch species kept as pets, partially because they are a very hardy species. Zebra Finches grow to about 4 inches (10 cm) tall and they weigh 17 to 19 grams at maturity. These little birds get their name from the black-and-white striped pattern on their head and upper chest which contrasts with a bright white belly and patches of chestnut brown on the cheeks and under the wings.

The Zebra Finch is also known as the spotted-sided finch or the chestnut-eared finch and it comes in several color variants such as an all-white mutation and a fawn-colored mutation. Zebra Finches are native to Australia and they are a social and active but also somewhat pushy and territorial breed. These finches do not sing particularly well but they do breed prolifically.

b.) Gouldian Finch (*Erythrura gouldiae*)

Also known as the Lady Gouldian Finch, this finch species is known for its bright coloration. These little birds have bright purple chests with yellow bellies that fade into white and various shades of green along the back. The head is black with orange or red coloration. This coloration is what gives the species its many nicknames including rainbow finch and purple-breasted finch. It is also sometimes called the painted finch, though this name actually belongs to a separate species.

The Gouldian Finch grows to about 5 inches (13 cm) tall and it weighs 16 to 17 grams at maturity. These finches are very hardy in captivity, though it may take them a little extra time to get used to their habitat. Gouldian Finches are considered a passive species which means that they tend to get along well with other finches. These finches do not sing very well and they can be tricky to breed.

c.) Society Finch (Lonchura striata domestica)

Also known as the Bengalese Finch (a reference to their Asian origins), the Society Finch is a small, hardy species of finch that tends to get along well with other finches. These birds grow to about 4 inches (10 cm) tall and they come in a variety of colors and patterns, though various shades of brown are most common. These birds sing very well and they are prolific breeders.

The song of the Society Finch is a little bit squeaky, sometimes with a rattle – males sing more than females and their songs are often similar to the male bird that raised them. The Society Finch is a domesticated species developed from an Asian species of finch, though it is not found anywhere in the wild. This species is highly social, often exhibiting group grooming and they will even act as foster parents, raising chicks from other species along with their own chicks.

d.) Star Finch (Neochmia ruficauda)

The Star Finch is one of the easiest finch species to identify because it has a greenish-yellow breast, an olive green back and throat with white spots, and a bright red face (though there are color mutations with yellow faces). These birds grow to about 4.25 inches (11 cm) and they weigh a maximum around 14 grams. Star Finches take a little bit of extra time to acclimate but, once they do, they are a very hardy species. These birds are also very passive so they get along well with other finches.

Star Finches have a rather quiet song, but it is very pleasant to listen to. This species originates in Australia and they are known for their calm, quiet, and peaceful nature. The Star Finch tends to live in medium- to large-sized flocks and they are very prolific breeders. These birds enjoy seeds and insects as the majority of their diet.

e.) Owl Finch (Taeniopygia bichenovii)

The Owl Finch is named for the owl-like colors and patterns it is known for. These birds have a brownish-gray body with black and white spotted wings, a dark tail, and a white upper chest. What really sets this species apart, however, is its bright white face which is rimmed in a thin black band with another black band running across the lower breast. These finches also have blue-gray beaks.

Owl Finches are a friendly and social breed – they are also fairly passive so they mix well with other species. These birds do take some time to acclimate but they are very hardy once they do and they are prolific breeders in captivity as well. The Owl Finch grows to 4 inches (10 cm) tall and weighs 15 to 17 grams at maturity. These birds are a little rarer than other species so they tend to be a bit more expensive to purchase.

f.) Strawberry Finch (*Amandava amandava*)

Also known as the Red Avadavat, the Strawberry Finch is a small finch species known for its bright red coloration and white spots. These birds grow to a height of 3.6 to 4 inches (9 to 10 cm) and they only weigh about 7 grams or so at maturity. Strawberry finches take time to acclimate but they are very hardy once they do and they are a long-lived species as well.

In addition to being known for its bright red color, the Strawberry Finch is also known for its excellent singing ability. These finches are a little tricky to breed, however, though their sexual dimorphism makes it very easy to distinguish males from females. Male Strawberry Finches have a lovely flute-like song and, while the female sings as well, it isn't as loud.

g.) Spice Finch (Lonchura punctulata)

The Spice Finch is also known as the Scaly-Breasted Munia due to the scale-like pattern on its chest. These finches are usually brown in color on the head, back, tail, and wings with a white chest decorated in a scale-like pattern. This species comes in thirteen subspecies and they are also known as the Nutmeg Finch, the Spotted Mannikin, or the Mascot Finch.

Spice Finches are a little larger than other finches, growing to 4.5 inches (11.5 cm) tall, but they still only weigh about 9.5 grams. These finches are very hardy and they are a passive species that mixes well with other finches. The downside is that these finches do not sing much and they are very difficult to breed. Still, if you are looking for a peaceful and social species, the Spice Finch is great.

Chapter Three: What to Know Before You Buy

    With what you now know about finches, you may have some idea whether or not these are the right pets for you. Before you make your decision, however, you should learn about some of the details of keeping finches as pets. In this chapter you will receive some important information about keeping finches together with other finches and other pets as well as an overview of the pros and cons for finches as pets. You will also receive a summary of the costs associated with keeping pet birds so you can determine whether or not you can financially support pet finches.

1.) How Many Should You Buy?

While there are some exceptions, finches are typically fairly social birds and they do best when kept in pairs or groups. The number of finches you purchase will depend on a variety of factors. For one thing, only passive species of finch do well when kept in large groups or in the same cage as other species. <u>Some of the most passive species of finch include the following</u>:

- Owl Finch
- Spice Finch
- Star Finch
- Society Finch
- Strawberry Finch
- Gouldian Finch

Finch species that are not on this list may get along with other finches if they are provided with enough space but they can become territorial. To reduce territoriality with finches, make sure the cage is very long to accommodate flight and ensure that each pair of birds has its own nesting box. You may also want to use larger toys and accessories in the cage to break up sightlines. <u>Some of the pushier or more territorial species of finch include the following</u>:

- Zebra Finch
- Lavender Finch
- Shaft-Tail Finch
- Aurora Finch
- European Goldfinch
- Green Singing Finch

Aside from keeping multiple finches in the same cage, it is best not to keep finches with other species. The only exception to this rule is with canaries as long as they are similar in size and temperament. Never keep finches with parrots, cockatoos, or other large pet birds.

2.) Can Finches Be Kept with Other Pets?

You probably do not need to be educated on the risks of keeping finches (or any pet bird) with other pets. While it may be possible to keep certain species of finch with other finches, you should not mix finches with other pet birds. Cats and some breeds of dog will chase or catch a finch if they get the chance so you also need to be very careful about keeping your finch cage closed securely at all times. If you choose to take your finches out of the cage to tame them, you should only do so in a room with the door closed and no other pets present.

3.) Ease and Cost of Care

Owning a pet can be expensive so before you make the commitment you need to be sure that you can cover the necessary costs. For pet finches you need to not only be able to pay for the birds themselves, but you also need to provide a safe and healthy habitat as well as a healthy diet. In this section you will receive an overview of the costs associated with purchasing and keeping finches as pets. If you cannot cover these costs, finches might not be the right pets for you.

a.) Initial Costs

The initial costs associated with keeping finches as pets include the cost of the birds themselves as well as the cage, cage accessories, toys, and grooming supplies. You will find an overview of these costs below as well as a chart depicting the estimated costs for keeping a single pair of finches as well as a group of four finches:

Purchase Price – The average cost for a single finch will vary depending on the species, the color mutation, and where you get it. Depending what type of finches you get, you should plan to spend $50 to $300 (£45 to £180) per pair.

Cage – The cost for a high-quality finch cage will vary greatly depending on the size, the type of cage, and the quality of the materials. Your best option is a large flight cage which could cost anywhere from $75 to as much as $500 or more (£68 to £450).

Cage Accessories – To properly outfit your finch cage you will need at least three food and water dishes as well as a nesting box, and several perches. The cost for these items can vary greatly but you should budget about $100 to $200 (£90 to £180) to be safe.

Toys – You really only need to keep 3 toys in your finch cage at any given time for a single pair of finches, though you should keep a variety of toys on hand so you can rotate them in and out to prevent boredom. Plan to spend about $50 (£45) on toys.

Grooming Supplies – Like many birds, finches enjoy taking baths so you will need to have a bird bath available in your finch cage. Other grooming supplies you might need include nail trimmers and styptic powder. The average cost you can expect to pay for these supplies is around $40 (£36).

Initial Costs for Finches		
Cost Type	1 Pair	2 Pairs

Purchase Price	$50 to $300 (£45 to £270)	$100 to $600 (£90 to £540)
Cage	$75 to $500 (£68 to £450)	$75 to $500 (£68 to £450)
Accessories	$100 to $200 (£90 to £180)	$100 to $200 (£90 to £180)
Toys	$50 (£45)	$100 (£90)
Grooming Supplies	$40 (£36)	$40 (£36)
Total	$315 to $1,090 (£284 to £981)	$415 to $1,440 (£374 to £1,296)

b.) **Monthly Costs**

The monthly costs associated with keeping finches as pets include the cost of bird food, nesting and bedding supplies, cleaning supplies, and veterinary care. You will find an overview of these costs below as well as a chart depicting the estimated costs for keeping a single pair of finches as well as two pairs of finches:

Bird Food – Feeding your finches a high-quality diet is the key to keeping your birds happy and healthy. Some finch owners choose to feed their birds a seed mix while others prefer pellet foods. In addition to your finches' staple diet you should also offer supplemental foods like fresh fruits and vegetables. The cost for finch food varies depending on quality but you should plan to spend about $20 (£9) on a large bag of bird food that will last you about a month for a single pair of finches. Add to that the cost of fresh and supplemental foods you should budget for about $40 (£36) per month on food.

Nesting/Bedding Supplies – In order for your finches to be able to build a nest you need to provide nesting materials like wood shavings and small twigs. Plan to spend about $15 (£13.50) on nesting supplies.

Cleaning Supplies – If you want to keep your finches healthy you need to maintain a clean cage. You won't need to buy cleaning supplies every month but you should budget a cost of about $10 (£9) per month on supplies.

Veterinary Care – Not all veterinarians are qualified to care for birds so you might have to find an exotics vet to take care of your finches. The average cost for this kind of veterinarian visit is about $50 (£45). You will not need to take your birds to the vet every month. If you take your finches to the vet twice a year and divide that cost over twelve months you should budget about $8 (£7.20) per month, per bird.

Additional Costs – In addition to all of these monthly costs you should plan for occasional extra costs like repairs to your canary cage, replacement toys, etc. Again, you won't have to cover these costs every month but you should budget about $10 (£9) per month to be safe.

Monthly Costs for Finches		
Cost Type	**1 Pair**	**2 Pairs**
Bird Food	$40 (£36)	$80 (£72)
Nesting/Bedding	$15 (£13.50)	$15 (£13.50)
Cleaning Supplies	$10 (£9)	$10 (£9)
Veterinary Care	$16 (£14.40)	$32 (£29)
Additional Costs	$10 (£9)	$10 (£9)
Total	$91 (£82)	$147 (£132)

4.) Pros and Cons of Finches

Before you decide whether or not finches are the right pet for you, you should familiarize yourself with both the advantages and disadvantages of finches as pets. <u>Below you</u>

will find a list of pros and cons for finches in general to help you make your decision:

Pros for Finches as Pets

- Finches come in many different species, colors, and patterns.
- Many finches sing beautiful songs, though it is mainly the males of each species that sing.
- Finches are generally small birds that do not require cages as large as parrots and other pet birds.
- Most finches are hardy and adaptable species as long as their basic needs are met.
- Many finch species are passive and social species that can be kept with other finches.
- For the most part, finches breed readily in captivity, though there are some exceptions.

Cons for Finches as Pets

- It is not recommended that you keep a single finch – they are best kept in pairs or groups, depending on the species.
- Some finch species can be very loud and boisterous, such as the Zebra Finch.
- Finches require an avian vet – this may cost more than a regular vet checkup for a dog or cat.

- Some finches can be very messy, flinging seed around the cage.
- Finches are generally not a pet bird that you can handle a lot, though some can be tamed with time.

Chapter Four: Purchasing Finches

At this point you should have a good idea whether or not finches are the right pet for you, but there is still some important practical information to consider. For example, do you need a permit to keep finches as pets and where will you buy your finches? You will find the answers to these questions and more in this chapter. You will also receive some helpful tips for choosing a responsible finch breeder and for picking out a healthy bird after you have chosen the right breeder. This is very important because you do not want to bring home a bird that is already sick or carrying some kind of disease.

1.) Do You Need a Permit?

Before you bring home any kind of new pet you need to make sure that there aren't any legal restrictions in your area. Some pets are illegal to keep without a permit or license, so you need to be very careful. In this section you will learn the basics about permit requirements for keeping finches as pets in the United States as well as the United Kingdom and other areas.

1.) U.S. Licensing Requirements

The United States has a lot of laws governing which animals are and are not legal to keep. In most cases, however, these laws apply to endangered or dangerous animals, not so much to pet birds. The one piece of legislation you will need to reference is the Migratory Bird Treaty Act which was passed in 1918. This act states that it is "illegal for anyone to take, possess, import, export, transport, sell, purchase, barter, or offer for sale, purchase, or barter, any migratory bird, or the parts, nests, or eggs of such a bird except under the terms of a valid permit issued pursuant to federal regulations".

The most important thing you need to take away from this is that it is illegal to keep birds that are native to the United States as pets unless you obtain a special permit.

This applies to a number of finch species including the American Goldfinch, the Purple Finch, and the House Finch. Fortunately, most of the finch species that are kept as pets are not native to the United States. This means that you can keep most finch species legally without a permit.

One more thing you need to be wary of with keeping finches as pets is that they need to be captive-bred. It is not legal to keep wild-caught birds as pets. If you need more information about keeping finches legally or about obtaining a permit for a wild-caught finch you will need to contact your local branch of the U.S Fish and Wildlife Service. You can find more information about importing and exporting pet birds here:

http://www.fws.gov/international/travel-and-trade/traveling-with-your-pet-bird.html#3

2.) U.K. Permit Requirements

The laws for keeping certain pets in the U.K. and Australia are very different than the laws in the United States. Just like in the U.S., it is illegal to keep dangerous and endangered animals as pets without a permit, but there are fewer pet regulations in the U.K. in general. You should not need a license or permit to purchase or keep pet finches because they are neither endangered nor native species to the U.K. The one permit you might need is called an animal movement license – this is the permit you'll need to import, export, or travel with your finches. This requirement is in place to prevent the spread of disease. It is primarily geared toward preventing rabies (the U.K. eradicated rabies a number of years ago) but it applies to other communicable diseases as well.

2.) Where to Buy Finches

Once you have determined whether it is legal to keep finches as pets in your area, your next step is to decide where you want to buy your finches. You may or may not be able to find pet finches at your local pet store and, even if you do, you might want to consider buying directly from a breeder instead. Below you will find some recommendations for finding a reputable finch breeder to ensure that your pet finch is healthy.

a. Tips for Finding a Finch Breeder

Even if you do not buy your finches from a pet store, it is not a bad place to start your search. If the store does carry finches, you can ask them where the birds came from and then contact the supplier for more information. If the store doesn't carry finches, you can ask around to see if they have any information about local breeders. You can also try asking around among your fellow bird lovers or simply perform an online search.

Once you've come up with a list of several finch breeders you want to take the time to vet them. If you are careful about weeding out the hobby breeders from the ones that know what they are doing you are more likely to end up with a healthy, well-bred bird. Keep in mind that finches come in a wide range of species, colors, and patterns, so breeders are likely to specialize in a particular type. It will help you to narrow your search if you decide ahead of time which kind of finch you want then you can focus only on breeders for that type.

After assembling and narrowing down your list to include just a handful of options, take the time to review the websites for each breeder. Look for important information about the breeder's experience with finches (especially with the species you have chosen) and with breeding birds in general – you should also check to make sure they have the appropriate breeding license, if required in your area. Any breeders that do not appear to have a solid background should be removed from your list before you move to the next step.

Once you've determined that the breeders on your list are qualified and experienced you should call them individually and ask them some important questions. When speaking directly to the breeder you can gain important information about their breeding practices to determine whether or not they really know what they are doing. Any breeder that refuses to answer questions or that cannot answer your questions fully and confidently should be removed from your list.

By this point you should have narrowed down your list to two or three breeders. The next step is to actually visit the breeding facilities to make sure that the breeder is actually doing what he says he is. Ask for a tour of the facilities to make sure that they are clean and well-kept – you should also ask to see the breeding stock to make sure that they are in good health and that they are good examples of the type you are seeking. After this visit you should be able to narrow down your options to just one breeder at which point you can actually purchase your finches or put down a deposit if the birds are not old enough to go home yet.

b. Finch Breeders in the United States

Because there are many different species of finches to choose from, you will probably have to do some extensive research to narrow down your options. To help you start the process of finding your finches you can perform an internet search or ask around for recommendations at your local pet store or vet clinic. Below you will find links to several finch breeders in the United States:

The Finch Farm. <http://www.thefinchfarm.com/>

The White Finch Aviary.
<https://lebeaupinson.wordpress.com/>

Acadiana Aviaries. <http://www.zebrafinch.com/>

Finches by Kristy. <http://www.finchesbykristy.com/>

Fabulous Finches.
<http://www.fabulousfinch.com/gouldians-for-sale.htm>

c. Finch Breeders in the United Kingdom

Finding finch breeders in the U.K. is not significantly different from finding them in the U.S. To help you get started, you will find links to several finch breeders in the United Kingdom below:

The Waxbill Finch Society.
<http://www.waxbillfinchsociety.org.uk/wfs_fs.html>
The Australian Finch Society.
<http://www.australianfinchsociety.co.uk/salesandwants.ht m>

Riverside Aviaries.
<http://www.riversideaviaries.co.uk/birds.htm>

Telford Bird Breeders.
<http://telfordbirdbreeders.co.uk/Bengalese-Finch.html>

3.) How to Select a Healthy Finch

Choosing a reputable finch breeder will help to ensure that the birds you bring home are well-bred but you still need to take certain steps to ensure that they are healthy as well. While it is certainly possible to buy a pet finch sight unseen, it is not recommended. Many finch species live for 10 years or more when properly cared for, so you want to make sure that your pet birds have the best start possible.

<u>Follow the steps below to make sure you come home from the breeder with a healthy finch</u>:

- Observe the bird from afar before approaching it – you want to make sure that it exhibits a healthy activity level and that it is able to sit on the perch properly.

- Examine the bird's body language – does it appear healthy and active? Does it seem to be overly shy or frightened of humans? Are there any visible signs of illness?

- If possible, watch the bird fly and eat to make sure that both of these functions can be performed normally without any problems.

- Check the state of the cage the birds are kept in – is it clean? Are the food/water bowls clean?

- Take a closer look at the individual finches to look for signs of illness – are its eyes bright and clear? Are its feathers puffed up? Are there patches of dirty or lost feathers?

- Once you've determined that there are no obvious signs of illness, take a moment to handle the bird if it will let you – use this opportunity to examine the bird more closely.

- Check the vent (the area under the tail) for cleanliness – if the area is dirty it could be a sign of diarrhea which is a sign of illness in birds.

- Examine the bird's feathers to make sure they have grown in properly and that they are the right color, pattern, or type that you prefer.

If everything about the bird appears to be healthy you can speak to the breeder about putting down a deposit or take the bird home immediately. Make sure to ask whether the bird comes with any sort of health guarantee or documentation that you might need.

Chapter Five: Caring for Finches

Now that you know a little bit more about the practicalities of being a bird owner you are ready to get into the specifics about keeping finches. In order to keep your finches happy and healthy you need to provide them with a safe habitat and a healthy diet. In this chapter you will receive detailed instructions about setting up your finch cage as well as tips for creating a healthy, balanced diet for your new pets. You will also receive tips about handling and taming your finches, should you choose to.

1.) Habitat Requirements

One of the most important things you need to do as a bird owner is to provide your finches with a safe and healthy habitat. Pet birds like finches spend most of their lives in their cage, so choosing the right cage is not a decision that should be taken lightly. In this section you will receive in-depth instructions regarding the selection and accessorizing of your finch cage.

a.) Minimum Cage Requirements

While some pet birds like parrots can exercise by climbing the walls of their cage, the only way finches can exercise is by flying. For this reason, it is important that you choose a fairly large cage for your finches and it needs to be longer than it is wide to accommodate for flight. If you are tempted to save money by purchasing a smaller cage, keep in mind that your finches will spend almost their entire lives in the cage – it is worth getting a bigger cage to make sure that your birds happy and healthy. Finches are not very large birds, so a cage that is roomy enough for several finches still won't be as large as a cage for a parrot or another bird would be – keep that in mind as well.

For a pair of finches, the minimum cage size is 30 inches long, 18 inches wide, and about 18 inches tall

(76x46x46 cm). This is the minimum recommendation for a single pair of finches in order to allow normal flight patterns. If you plan to keep more than two finches in the same cage, you will want it to be a little bit bigger. The best thing you can do for your finches is to buy something called a flight cage. A flight cage is simply a cage that is large enough and long enough to allow for normal flight.

While size is the most important factor for your finch cage, there are a few other things you need to consider. For example, the spacing between the bars on your bird cage is very important. You want to spacing to be no more than ½ inch (though ¼ inch is better) – if the spacing is any larger your finches could get their heads caught between the bars or they could even escape. Bars spaced too far apart could also impact your finch's ability to perch and climb on the sides of the cage.

Another factor you want to consider is the bottom of the cage. Your finches will spend most of their time flying around the cage and resting on perches, but you do need to think about the bottom of the cage as well. It is best to find a cage that has a slide-out tray at the bottom to facilitate easy cleaning. You can line this tray with newspaper or bird cage liners and then just throw it away and replace it for quick cleaning. You may want to avoid cages that have wire mesh or bars on the bottom because these can injure your finch's feet and lead to a condition called bumblefoot.

b.) Cage Accessories and Toys

In addition to providing your finches with a cage large enough for flying, you also need to provide certain cage accessories. You should also be intentional about how you arrange the cage. <u>The most important cage accessories for pet finches include the following</u>:

- Food and water dishes
- Perches
- Bathing tub
- Nesting box
- Nesting materials
- Cuttlebone
- Toys

Food and Water Dishes

Food and water should be available to your birds at all times and the number of dishes you need will depend on the number of finches you are keeping. If you have more than one pair of finches, you'll need a separate food dish for each pair as well as one or two water dishes. The dishes should be made of sturdy materials because your finches will perch on them to eat and drink – stainless steel is the best option because it is the easier to clean and it won't harbor bacteria. Ceramic dishes are another good option, though they are heavier and might be more difficult to mount in the cage.

Many finch owners recommend having multiple separate bowls for different types of food – one for water, one for pellets or seed mix, and one for fresh foods.

Perches

Though finches spend a lot of time flying, they need access to perches when they want to rest. You should provide your finches with at least three different perches made from different materials like natural wood or wooden dowels. Avoid plastic perches because they can get scratched up and then might harbor bacteria. Look for perches that offer some kind of texture so the birds will be able to grip it – do not use perches that are completely smooth. You should also avoid perches that are too rough such as sandpaper perches – these can injure your finches' feet. Perches should be about ¼ to ½ inch in diameter for finches.

Bathing Tub

Finches like to bathe because it helps them to remove debris from their feathers and it helps to keep their skin moisturized as well. For small birds like the finch you can keep a bird bath in the cage so the bird can bathe whenever it likes. The bird bath should consist of a shallow, heavy bowl filled with 1 or 2 inches of water – the water should not be deeper than the height of your finch. Keep an eye on the bird bath and refresh the water after each bath. You can go with a bird bath that sits on the bottom of the cage or you can go with one that mounts to the side of the cage. It is simply a matter of preference.

Nesting Box

Many species of finch breed fairly readily in captivity so you should provide them with a nesting box and nesting materials. The best nesting boxes for finches are made from wood or bamboo – these materials are soft enough that they won't injure your canary's feet if they get caught. You should mount the nesting box to the back or side of the cage near the top so it doesn't get in the way of your finches' natural flight path.

Nesting Materials

In addition to providing your finches with a nesting box, you need to provide them with an assortment of nesting materials to use in building their nests in the box. Mount a tray or pan of nesting materials to the side of the cage and fill it with soft wood shavings, small twigs, and other soft materials. Make sure the tray you use to hold the materials is sturdy enough to support the weight of your finch and it is best made from easy-to-clean materials like ceramic or stainless steel.

Cuttlebone

Mounting a cuttlebone on the side of your finch cage is highly recommended. Not only will your finch use it as a kind of plaything, but it is also a valuable source of calcium for your bird – this is particularly important for female finches to help them with healthy egg development. As your finch nibbles on the bone it will also help to keep his beak trimmed down.

Toys

In addition to being very active birds, many finch species also have a playful side so you'll want to provide your birds with an assortment of toys. Provide your finches with at least three different types of toys and space them throughout the cage so they don't interfere with their flight. Some good options for toys include rope toys, stainless steel bells, swings, and more. Just make sure that your finch toys are made from nontoxic materials that are easy to clean. You may want to keep a large selection of toys and rotate them in and out of the cage to prevent boredom.

Now that you know what accessories your finches need you can start to think about how you will arrange the cage to accommodate all of them. Finches are active birds so the most important thing you need to remember is that space for flight is an absolute necessity. You do not want to overcrowd the cage with toys and accessories which might limit their flight. Try to space your accessories out to leave plenty of open space. One way to do this is to stagger the spacing of your perches and other accessories. For example, you might place two perches along the sides of the cage on either end and then place another set of perches on the front and back walls of the cage higher up. By staggering the perches this way, you leave enough room between them for your finches to fly back and forth.

c.) Building Your Own Cage

Because finches are generally very active they require a large flight cage to remain happy and healthy. Unfortunately, large bird cages can be fairly expensive – especially if you buy one made from high-quality materials. For this reason, many finch owners choose to build their own cages. A DIY finch cage gives you the ability to customize the size and shape of the cage to fit the space you have available in your home. Plus, you can design it to suit the preferences of your finches.

The best materials to use for a DIY finch cage are plywood and welded wire mesh. You can use a sheet of plywood for the top and bottom of the cage then construct the walls out of 1-by-2 inch boards or something similar. You can then use the welded wire mesh to enclose the cage.

You also have the option of building wooden accessories like perches and nesting boxes directly into the framework of the cage. Just be sure that all wood surfaces are properly sanded to avoid injury and make sure that the gauge of your welded wire mesh is large enough that your finches' toes won't get caught.

d.) Lighting and Temperature

The size and shape of your finch cage is incredibly important, but you also have to think about the location of the cage as well. Finches are adaptable to different temperatures because different species come from different habitats. For the most part, however, they prefer warm environments no more than 78°F (25.5°C). The best daytime temperature range for finches is between 60°F and 70°F (15.5°C to 21°C) with nighttime temperatures dropping no lower than about 40°F (4.5°C).

You may also want to keep an eye on the humidity in your finch cage. Most finch species come from fairly temperate areas so you don't need to keep the humidity too high – something in the 50% to 60% range should be sufficient. You can keep the humidity in your finch cage up by misting it with warm water from a spray bottle daily or you can set up a drip system. Higher humidity levels may be beneficial for breeding and for making sure that the eggs do not dry out before hatching.

Place your finch cage in a location that won't be affected by drafts – this means you'll have to keep it away from air conditioning vents, windows, and doors to the outside. The best location for a finch cage is one where the temperature is stable and there is a moderate amount of activity – don't make your finch cage the center of attention in a very busy room because it could cause stress. If your finches start to become stressed, you can try covering the cage with a blanket or cage cover. For the most part, however, it is not necessary to cover your bird cage at night like you would with other bird species.

2.) Feeding Finches

In the wild, finches follow a varied diet of different types of seeds, small insects, and sometimes young sprouts. Unfortunately, many finches kept in captivity are offered a seed-only diet which can be deficient in essential nutrients. To make sure that your finches are happy and healthy, you need to be intentional about creating a diet that is properly balanced in all of the essential nutrients your finches need. In this section you will receive an overview of the nutritional needs for finches as well as some helpful tips for creating a healthy diet for your pet finches.

a.) Nutritional Needs of Finches

In order to keep your finches healthy, you need to understand the basics about their nutritional needs and design a diet that will meet them. In the wild, finches feed largely on a wide variety of seeds, so that is what you should feed your pet finches. It is important to remember, however, that seeds are not the only things wild finches eat – they also feed on small insects and certain fruits, vegetables, and berries. For this reason, you need to feed your finches a diet that consists primarily of seeds but is supplemented with other foods.

For most finches, about 60% to 70% of the diet should be made up of seeds but there are some other important foods to include as well. In addition to seeds, your finches should receive small amounts of fresh fruits and vegetables as well as some cooked grains and other supplementary foods. You may also want to give your finches some dietary supplements to help round out their nutrition. Just make sure that your seed mix is always available because finches will eat up to 30% of their bodyweight in food daily.

In addition to feeding your finches a well-balanced diet, you should also make sure that fresh water is always available. Not only is fresh water important for keeping your birds hydrated but it will also help to ensure healthy digestion. Most finches will drink water from a small bowl or dish mounted on the side of the cage. Just keep an eye on it and refresh the water daily, cleaning the bowl when you do to get rid of food particles and germs.

b.) Types of Food

In the wild, finches feed on a variety of different seeds, but mostly grass seeds. You can certainly put together your own seed mix if you want to, but it will be easier to just purchase a high-quality finch seed mix. Purchasing a commercial seed mix is usually the easier option, but you do need to be careful about which blend you choose. Some seed mixes are too high in fats and carbohydrates but low in protein and other nutrients. Look for a seed mix that provides a good balance of nutrients without being too high in fat.

Another problem you might run into with commercial seed mixes is that your finches could simply pick out their favorite seeds, leaving the rest untouched. For example, many finches favor millet seed and they will pick them out of the seed mix. If you are worried about this happening to you, consider buying a finch pellet food instead of a seed blend. Bird food pellets are made primarily from seed, but the ingredients are all blended together which means that your bird can't pick out certain seeds that he likes. These pellet foods also contain supplemental ingredients like grains and proteins to ensure well-rounded nutrition for your finches.

While a seed mix or finch pellet is the best option for your birds' staple diet, 30% to 40% of their diet should consist of other foods. Your finches will get plenty of healthy nutrition from fresh fruits and vegetables as well as whole grain bread, cooked rice or sweet potato, sprouted seeds, and mealworms or other insects. You might also want to consider offering your finches a cuttlebone to make sure they get the minerals they need.

Fresh Vegetables (offer daily)

- Beets
- Bean Sprouts
- Broccoli*
- Carrot

- Carrot Tops
- Corn
- Collard Greens
- Cucumber
- Dandelion Greens
- Kale
- Lettuce

- Parsley
- Peas
- Pumpkin
- Spinach*
- Sweet Potato
- Yams
- Zucchini

*Only offer these foods once or twice a week because they could interfere with calcium uptake.

Fresh Fruits (3x per week)

- Apple
- Apricots
- Banana
- Blueberries
- Kiwi

- Grapes
- Oranges
- Peaches
- Pears
- Raspberries

Grains and Starch (2x per week)

- Whole grain bread
- Whole wheat bread
- Cooked brown rice
- Cook sweet potato

- Cooked white potato
- Soaked/sprouted seeds

Protein (2x per week)

- Cooked chicken egg

- Mealworms

Supplements

Fresh fruits and vegetables will help to round out your finches' nutrition but you should also provide certain supplements to make sure their needs for certain vitamins and minerals are being met. One option is to provide your finches with a cuttlefish bone, also known as a cuttlebone – this is a great source of calcium. Many finch owners also provide their birds with oyster grit. Oyster grit contains both calcium and phosphorus, plus it can help your bird to digest fibrous foods and seeds.

You can also find multivitamin powders that you can mix directly into your finches' water but it is a good idea to ask your vet first to make sure you aren't over-supplementing your birds. It is possible to have too much of a good thing and overdosing on certain nutrients could be harmful for your finches.

Soaked and Sprouted Seeds

Soaked seeds can be considered an occasional treat for finches, though they are an essential food for feeding hens and newly weaned hatchlings. Large seeds like wheat, cracked corn, buckwheat, and safflower are usually too much for finches to handle but soaking them makes them easier to eat – it actually helps to start breaking down the complex carbohydrates to make them more digestible. Soak seeds for at least 24 hours and rinse then strain them well before offering them to your finches.

Sprouted seeds are not the same thing as soaked seeds and not all seeds can be sprouted. Mung beans are the easiest seeds to sprout and they are considered very palatable for finches and other birds. You can also use soy beans but most birds do not like alfalfa sprouts. To sprout seeds, place no more than a quarter cup in a clean glass jar then fill with tap water. Let the jar set for 24 hours at room temperature then rinse and drain. Rinse and drain the seeds once daily until the seeds have sprouted – discard them if they develop a mold or foul odor at any time. Sprouted seeds can be kept fresh in the refrigerator for up to two weeks before discarding them.

c.) Feeding Tips and Amount to Feed

The best way to feed your finch is to keep one or more seed dishes in the cage. Make sure not to fill the dishes too full because your finches could soil the dishes, ruining the food, and you don't want to waste too much of it. Check your seed dishes at least twice daily to make sure they are clean and refill them as needed with fresh pellets. To offer your finches fresh fruits and vegetables, place them in a separate dish or clip them to the side of the cage.

In terms of how much food you should be offering your finches, recommendations vary. As a general guideline, start with 1 to 2 level teaspoons of seed or pellets per bird per day. If you have more than one pair of finches in the same cage, make sure there is at least one food dish per pair and space them out so each bird can eat in peace. If you choose to use finch pellets, refer to the feeding recommendations on the package. You want to avoid overfeeding your finches because birds are prone to obesity if they are overfed.

If you start out feeding your finch seeds, it may be difficult for you to switch him over to a pelleted diet later. The best way to do this is to slowly wean your finches off the seeds while making sure that pellet foods are constantly available. If you choose this method, you should do it over a period of 6 to 8 weeks to make sure that you don't make any major changes to their diet too quickly. You can also try mixing a little bit of the pelleted food in with your seeds to get your finches used to it.

When feeding your finches fresh fruits and vegetables it is essential that you clean them properly. In addition to washing your produce, remove any pits or seeds and chop the foods into small, manageable pieces before offering them to your birds. It is a good idea to have a separate food dish for fresh foods because if you put it in with the seed it could encourage mold or fungus growth when the seeds get wet.

d. Harmful Foods to Avoid

Though many so-called "people foods" like fresh fruits and whole grain bread can be good for your finches, many are not. Avoid feeding your finches dairy products, sugary foods, salty foods, raw potato, beans, and canned foods. It is also important to note that while certain vegetables like lettuce and cabbage are not necessarily bad for your bird, they are very high in water and offer relatively little in the way of nutritional value. There are also some foods that are considered toxic or harmful for birds – you will find them listed here below:

- Asparagus
- Avocado
- Alcohol
- Caffeine
- Chocolate
- Cocoa
- Dried Beans
- Eggplant
- Fruit Pits

- Fruit Seeds
- Poultry Feed
- Raw Egg
- Rhubarb
- Tobacco
- Tomato
- Milk
- Moldy Foods
- Mushrooms

**It is also important to note that even safe foods need to be clean and free from mold. Do not feed your finch anything that is damp, moldy, or anything less than fresh.

3.) Handling and Taming Finches

While some pet bird species like parrots and cockatoos can spend time outside the cage, finches generally live most of their lives in the cage – they are not the kind of pet bird that you will handle very often. If you are determined to train and tame your finches, however, there are certain species that work best for this sort of thing. In this section you will learn some basic tips for taming and handling finches as well as information about trimming your finches' nails and wings.

a. Tips for Taming Finches

If you want to have a tamed finch that will allow you to handle it, you should start with a very young bird from a certain species. You should choose a species that is naturally very calm and friendly – the Zebra Finch is generally a good choice. Once you've picked your finch you should start with a daily training routine consisting of two 10- to 15-minute sessions. Make sure to hold these training sessions at the same time each day so your bird gets used to the routine. You should also spend plenty of time in the room with your finches so they get used to acting normally in your presence.

Before you even handle your finch for the first time you need to get it used to you. Start by placing your hands in the cage, holding them out flat like a perch. You may even want to place a treat in your hand to encourage your bird to land there. Keep your hand steady and just wait for your bird to come around – do not chase him around the cage. If he doesn't come to you after 10 or 15 minutes, remove your hands and try again later. In terms of training, some finches can be taught to perform simple tricks. Again, it will take a great deal of time and patience to achieve this goal, so be prepared for that before you begin.

The proper way to handle a pet finch is to place your hand gently on its back and wrap your fingers around the bird's body with your thumb and forefinger circled around the head and neck for support. Be careful not to hold the finch too tightly but maintain a firm enough grip that it won't be able to get away. If you plan to handle your bird on a regular basis you need to be able to recognize signs of stress. You should only handle your finch for short periods of time and as soon as he starts to get uncomfortable it is best to put him back in the cage. Signs of stress in finches may include flattening the feathers against the body, panting with the mouth open, or moving away from you.

b.) Trimming Your Finch's Nails

Trimming your finch's nails is a necessary task but it can also be a challenging one. For one thing, some finches simply do not like being held so if your bird isn't tamed and used to handling, trimming his nails could become quite the ordeal. When it comes time to trim your bird's nails, hold him using the method described in the last section. Carefully maneuver your hand to hold one toe between your thumb and forefinger then clip just the very tip of the nail. Keep in mind that each nail contains a quick - that is the blood vessel that supplies blood to the nail. If you clip the nail too short you could sever the quick and that will be painful for your finch.

Even if you are very careful when cutting your finch's nails there is always the risk that you might cut the quick. If you do, the nail could start bleeding profusely and that is something you want to get under control right away. You can stop the bleeding quickly by dipping the nail in cornstarch, flour, or styptic powder. Always keep one of these materials on hand when you clip your bird's nails, just in case you need it. If you aren't confident in your ability to cut your finch's nails, try having a veterinarian show you how.

c.) Clipping a Finch's Wings

Keeping a pet finch is not like keeping a pet parrot. While pet parrots and other larger birds can be allowed out of the cage, finches generally spend most of their lives in the cage. The only reason you would need to clip a bird's wings is if it is allowed out of the cage and you want to limit its flight. For finches, however, being able to fly is incredibly important because they are very active birds. If you clip your finch's wings you would impede his ability to fly and it could have a negative impact on his health and overall wellbeing.

Chapter Six: Breeding Finches

Not only are finches beautiful and active little birds, but many of them are also prolific breeders. In fact, you may not need to do anything at all in order to encourage your finches to breed – just provide them with a nest box, some nesting material, and they are good to go! If you want to learn more about how finch breeding works to increase the chances of your own finches breeding, you will find that information and more in this chapter. Keep in mind that different finch species have slightly different breeding habits – the information in this chapter applies to finches in general so you may need to do a bit of extra research.

1.) *Basic Finch Breeding Info*

If you think that breeding your finches sounds like a great idea you may be glad to know that many finch species breed readily in captivity without any prompting. In order to increase the chances of your finches breeding, take a moment to learn the basics about bird breeding in general. In this section you will receive some basic information about finch breeding including tips for telling the sexes apart as well as information about courtship behavior and nest building behavior exhibited by finch species.

a.) Sexual Dimorphism

In order to be successful in breeding finches you need to pair a male and a female of the same species together. If you are new to bird keeping, you may be concerned about the challenge of telling males apart from females. For the most part, however, finches are sexually dimorphic – this means that there are significant physical differences between the sexes. The Gouldian Finch and the Strawberry finches are two examples of sexually dimorphic species. In many cases, male finches are more brightly colored than females. Male finches also tend to sing more than females – females may chirp and cheep, but they do not exhibit the same singing ability as a male finch.

Though many finch species are sexually dimorphic, sometimes these differences only become apparent during the breeding season. For example, the Strawberry Finch cock looks very similar to the hen except during the breeding season when his colors brighten. It is also important to note that there are some sexually monomorphic finch species as well – species that do not show any significant physical differences between the sexes. This is true of Society Finches, Spice Finches, and Owl Finches. In cases like this you may need to study the singing habits of the finches to tell the sexes apart.

b.) Courtship Behavior

In most cases, male finches become sexually active earlier than females do. In the wild, this gives the male finch time to find a suitable nesting site before he starts working to attract a mate. Male finches engage in a number of courtship behaviors to attract a female finch, generally aiming for a finch of the same species. In captivity, however, it is not uncommon for male finches to court females of different species. It also sometimes happens that the female makes the first move, encouraging the male finch to sing to her – this happens with Star Finches.

When it comes to courtship behavior, the male finch usually exhibits a combination of song and dance. Different species exhibit slightly different courtship behaviors. Finches that dance while they sing incorporate a variety of movements including bowing, hopping, shaking the head, puffing out the chest, and standing tall. If the female accepts the advances of the male, you will notice signs of pair bond formation such as sleeping or perching together – the pair may also be seen preening or grooming each other.

In the wild, the breeding season for finches begins in the spring, though many finches breed freely in captivity. In the wild, male finches may begin to prepare for breeding a few weeks before the females as winter is just ending. If you keep a male and female canary together, the male may start to chase the female around the cage at this time. You may need to keep a close eye on your finches at this point because the male can become aggressive. In many cases, however, it is recommended that you condition the sexes separately before introducing them for breeding.

To condition your finches for breeding, you will need to feed them a high-protein diet. Female finches will also need some extra calcium in their diet to help with egg formation. As you condition your finches, look for signs that they are ready to mate. In female finches, building a nest is the best indicator that she is ready to breed. For males, courtship behavior may include feeding the female and "kissing" her. If the sexes are separated, the male may make visual displays in addition to singing. You will know that the two are ready to mate when the female acknowledges the displays of the male – she will indicate this by crouching down to allow mating to occur.

c.) Nest Building

If you plan to breed your finches, it is best to keep them in separate cages until they are both ready for breeding. In females, the sign that she is ready for breeding is that she will build a nest. For the best results, you should house the female in the cage you want to use as your breeding cage so you do not have to move her or the nest after it has been built. The ideal dimensions for a finch breeding cage are 18x11x14 inches (46x28x36 cm). Provide the female with a wicker or wooden nesting box and a pan of nesting materials. Recommended nesting materials include soft wood shavings, small twigs, and other soft bedding materials.

2.) The Finch Breeding Process

When it comes to the actual mating process, finch breeding usually occurs very soon after the pair are introduced – you shouldn't have to do anything to encourage the two to breed. Just be sure that your finches are the right age for breeding before you begin the process. Sexual maturity for finches typically occurs around 6 to 9 months of age, though it could be sooner for some male finches. Some finch breeders recommend that female finches should be at least 1-year-old for breeding and male canaries should be no more than 5 years old.

While preparing your finches for breeding you should feed them a healthy diet with rich foods. For females, you want to make sure that she gets enough fats and oils to prevent constipation and egg binding – adding a little bit of olive oil or wheat germ oil to her seed should help with this. Once the pair are both ready for breeding you can introduce the male to the female's cage – do not do it the other way around.

After a successful mating, the female will lay one egg per day until she is finished. The number of eggs per clutch will vary from one finch species to another, though the average is 3 to 8 eggs. Once the eggs have been laid the female will incubate them for about 13 to 14 days before they hatch. In some cases, you may notice the female taking a bath the day of or before hatching. When she returns to the nest she will wet the bedding which will help to soften the eggs in preparation for hatching. When the chicks are ready to hatch they will start by chipping a small hole in the side of the egg and then keep chipping away until the egg splits open.

When finch chicks first hatch they are almost completely naked and wet. The chicks' eyes will be closed and their beaks will be soft so they are completely dependent on the hen for care. The chicks will likely subsist off of the remainder of their yolk sac for half a day or so but they will need to be fed within 24 hours of hatching. In many cases, both the male and female finch care for the chicks, though some recommend removing the male from the cage after breeding just to be safe.

To make sure that your finch chicks get enough to eat you can start offering nestling food or you can make your own using mashed hardboiled eggs with water-soaked whole wheat bread. The female will continue to feed and care for the chicks until they are about 21 days old at which point they will leave the nest and begin to live independently. When the chicks are fully weaned they should be separated from the parents.

Chapter Seven: Keeping Finches Healthy

    While providing your finches with a healthy diet and a clean cage are a great way to keep your birds healthy, there may come a time when your finches get sick anyway. If this happens it is important to take decisive action in identifying the symptoms of the disease so you can take your bird to the avian vet and tell him what is going on. The sooner you take note of the symptoms and seek treatment for your finches, the better their chances are of making a full recovery. In this chapter you will find an overview of some of the diseases most commonly seen in finches so you can identify them early.

1.) Common Health Problems

Finches can be active and entertaining pets but, like any pet, they have the potential to get sick even if you take care of them to the best of your ability. If you want to make sure that your finches get the care they need, you would be wise to familiarize yourself with some of the most common health problems known to affect these birds. You will find a list of the most common conditions known to affect finches below and, in the following pages, you will receive an overview of these conditions including causes, symptoms, and treatment options.

Some of the common conditions known to affect finches may include the following:

- Air Sac Mites
- Aspergillosis
- Bumblefoot
- Coccidiosis
- Egg Binding

- Feather Cysts
- Feather Loss
- Overgrown Nails
- Scaly Face Mites
- Tapeworms

In the following pages you will receive an overview of each of these conditions including their clinical signs and symptoms, methods for diagnosis, treatment options and prognosis information.

Air Sac Mites

Respiratory problems are not uncommon in pet birds and one of the most frequently seen respiratory issues is related to a parasite infection known as air sac mites. Air sac mites can infiltrate the bird's entire respiratory tract and the severity of the infection can vary greatly. Birds with mild infections may not show any signs but severe infections may produce symptoms including trouble breathing, wheezing or clicking sounds, open-mouth breathing, excessive salivation, and bobbing the tail. Finches with air sac mites often stop singing and many exhibit reduced activity and puffed feathers.

Unfortunately, diagnosing a live bird with air sac mites can be difficult. In some cases, the mites might be visible to the naked eye, though a microscope is usually needed to make a diagnosis after a tracheal swab. This disease can be transmitted through close contact with an infected bird and through airborne particles. It can also be passed through contaminated food or drinking water so it is important that you quarantine your finches from other birds if it displays signs of air sac mites.

There are some treatment options available for air sac mites but you need to be very careful about choosing the right treatment. The signs that indicate air sac mites overlap with a number of other diseases so you need to make sure you have an accurate diagnosis before you start treatment. For example, vitamin A deficiency presents with symptoms very similar to air sac mites. Medications are available to treat the disease, though dosage can be tricky and many birds die from air sac mites.

Aspergillosis

Another common respiratory problem seen in pet birds like finches is called aspergillosis. This is a disease caused by a fungus and it is a slow-growing infection that can cause serious tissue damage throughout the body. Unfortunately, there is little physical evidence of a problem until the disease has progressed and the damage to the internal organs becomes severe. Not only is this disease difficult to detect, but it can also be very challenging to treat and to cure.

Aspergillosis can affect both the upper and lower respiratory tract. This fungus can be found in many environments but it doesn't typically become a problem until the bird's immune system becomes compromised by something else. Chronic stress, poor husbandry, and other respiratory irritants can increase a bird's risk for contracting this fungal infection. Once the bird gets sick, curing the infection can take a long time.

Because aspergillosis frequently presents without symptoms it can be difficult to diagnose. Your vet will likely recommend a complete blood count (CBC), an x-ray to check for lesions, and a tracheal wash to detect the presence of the fungus in the respiratory tract. Treatment options include oral or intravenous antifungal medications which must be taken over an extended period of time. Unfortunately, treatment is often ineffective unless the bird's immune system is very strong. This is fairly uncommon, however, because the disease tends to attack birds with compromised immune systems. If you do manage to cure the disease it is important that you maintain good hygiene and a healthy diet to prevent the disease from recurring or spreading.

Bumblefoot

Bumblefoot is a condition that can occur in any bird species but it is most commonly seen in captive rather than wild species. In many cases, the first symptom to be seen is swelling of the toes, feet, or joints, often with accompanied lameness. The affected bird may also be unwilling to land or perch normally and it might not be able to grasp the perch with both of its feet.

There are three stages of the bumblefoot disease beginning with the first stage in which pink-colored calluses or abrasions appear on the feet. These calluses are most commonly caused by perches that are too rough or too hard. The second stage of the disease involves the appearance of sores or lesions which can become inflamed or infected. During the third stage, the sores may turn dark blue or black and the foot and/or affected toes can become severely distorted and permanent damage may occur.

The treatment for bumblefoot is multi-focused. You need to thoroughly clean the cage including all of the perches and toys. Remove any rough or unclean perches and make sure that those left are suitable in texture and circumference. In cases where infection has set in, antibiotic medications or ointments may be prescribed. Soaking the affected foot in an Epsom salt bath may also help.

Coccidiosis

Coccidiosis is a type of parasite infection caused by a protozoan parasite known as Eimeria. When the parasite is transferred from one bird to another it takes up residence in the host's intestinal tract where it reproduces rapidly. This can lead to swelling in the intestines as well as intestinal bleeding. In cases where the condition goes untreated, it can lead to damage to the intestine which can contribute to the malabsorption of nutrients.

Though coccidiosis is most commonly seen in wild birds, it can easily be passed to pet birds as well. The disease is most likely to develop in cages where proper hygiene is not maintained – the parasite tends to thrive in poor and cramped conditions when the bird's immune system is already weakened by stress or by some other kind of illness or injury.

Unfortunately, many birds infected with coccidiosis do not show symptoms until the condition progresses and the bird becomes extremely stressed. Some of the symptoms of this condition may include weight loss, diarrhea, bloody stools, dehydration, and lethargy. The most common treatment option is the use of antibiotic medications such as Sulfonamide. The cage also needs to be thoroughly cleaned and kept clean to prevent re-infestation.

Egg Binding

Egg binding is a condition that can occur in any female bird and it is very dangerous and frequently fatal. This condition occurs when the egg fails to pass through the reproductive system at the normal rate. Female canaries can develop this condition regardless of the presence of a male since birds still lay eggs whether or not they are fertilized. Another dangerous and related condition is dystocia – this occurs when an obstruction prevents the female bird from laying the egg.

There are a number of factors which can increase your finch's risk for egg binding. Egg binding is particularly common in small birds like finches and repeated breeding (as well as breeding too young or out of season) can also be a factor. Egg binding is common in very young and very old birds, plus it can be affected by issues with malnutrition or poor overall health.

Egg binding is incredibly serious and frequently fatal so it is important that you are able to recognize the signs. Symptoms of egg binding may include abdominal straining, bobbing the tail, drooping wings, depression, loss of appetite, leg paralysis, distended abdomen, difficulty breathing, and sudden death. If you suspect egg binding, seek veterinary care immediately for your finch.

Feather Cysts

In the same way that humans can develop ingrown hairs, finches can develop feather cysts. Feather cysts form when the growing feather is malformed within the follicle (the part located under the skin) – it happens when the growing feather is unable to protrude through the skin so it curls up inside the follicle. This produces an oval-shaped or elongated swelling that can develop anywhere on the wing, though they are most common near the primary feathers. Finches can also develop feather cysts on the body.

Feather cysts may be small and minor at first but as they grow they can accumulate a yellowish-white keratin material that fills the cyst. Cysts can develop as a result of several factors including bacterial and viral infections, trauma, malnutrition, self-mutilation, and other problems related to feather growth. If the feather cyst is very small, it can sometimes be squeezed out. This is not the ideal treatment, however, because the cyst may reform. Feather cysts have the potential to bleed profusely so they are best handled by a qualified avian veterinarian. Surgical removal may be the only option in some cases.

Feather Loss

In finches and other related species, stress is the most common cause for feather loss. When your finch becomes stressed due to an aggressive cage mate, poor hygiene, or an unhealthy diet he may start plucking out his own feathers. Another potential cause for feather loss is parasite infection. Some birds also experience feather loss as the result of an iodine deficiency, though this is more common in Gouldian finches than in other species. If the feather loss is limited to the head, it is most likely due to aggression by other birds or a mite infection.

Overgrown Nails

Finches that are kept in captivity need to have their nails trimmed once in a while because they will not become worn down naturally as much as they would in the wild. If your finches' nails become overgrown, it could affect their ability to perch normally and the nails could grow so long that they begin to curl under and may puncture the skin on the feet. Overgrown nails in finches can also get stuck in nesting or bedding material – in extreme cases the bird could die if it gets stuck hanging upside down.

The best way to prevent overgrown nails in finches is to check them about once a week. Some finch species will need to have their nails trimmed more often than others. For example, Zebra Finches have nails that grow very slowly so they will not need to be trimmed as often as a Society Finch's nails might. When trimming your finches' nails, use sharp scissors and just cut off the sharp tip. Do not cut the nail too short or you could sever the quick (the blood supply to the nail) – this could hurt the bird and it may bleed profusely. If this happens, dip the nail in styptic powder to stop the bleeding.

Scaly Face Mites

Mites belonging to the genus *Knemidokoptes* are common referred to as "scaly mites" and they can affect the legs and face of multiple bird species. When scaly mites affect the legs it is sometimes called Tassel Foot. Scaly mites are particularly common in small birds like finches and they typically cause scaly, crusty white or gray lesions on the non-feathered skin on the beak, legs, and feet. Foot lesions are particularly common in finches, though they can also appear around the eyes and vent.

The parasites known as scaly mites typically spend their entire life cycles on the bird they are inhabiting. The mites burrow into the top layer of skin, forming tunnels they can travel through. The mites can be transmitted from one bird to another through direct contact – they can also be transferred to un-feathered chicks. If the bird has a suppressed immune system it has a greater susceptibility to contracting the disease.

There are several treatment options available for scaly mites but the most effective treatment is Ivermectin. This treatment is usually administered at 10-day intervals for 2 to 6 treatments. Ivermectin can be applied directly to the skin or it can be taken orally or injected. In addition to treatment with Ivermectin, the cage and all accessories need to be cleaned and disinfected.

Tapeworms

Tapeworms are a type of internal parasite that most commonly affects birds that are kept outdoors. These parasites can be transmitted to your finches if they eat an infected insect or through contact with contaminated feces. Once the tapeworm makes it into the bird's digestive tract it starts to leech nutrients, causing the bird to develop malnutrition. As the tapeworm grows and multiplies it can also produce a physical blockage of the intestinal tract which can become fatal for the bird.

Unfortunately, many birds affected by tapeworms do not show any outward symptoms until the malnutrition becomes fairly advanced. In some cases, however, you can actually see shed tapeworms in the bird's droppings if you look closely. A fecal exam is the best method for diagnosing a tapeworm infection and once your bird is diagnosed your vet will prescribe an anti-parasitic medication. These medications can be administered orally or through injection depending on the severity of the condition.

2.) Preventing Illness

Now that you know a little bit more about the various diseases known to affect finches you can keep an eye out for the common signs and symptoms. In addition to this, however, there are some other steps you can take to prevent illness. The most important thing you need to do is to keep your bird cage clean. <u>Below you will find an overview of recommended daily, weekly, and monthly cleaning tasks for your finch cage:</u>

Daily Cleaning Tasks

On a daily basis you should replace your finch cage liner, clean your food and water dishes, and clean and refresh your bird bath. You may also want to clean your bird toys and accessories if they become soiled. Because your cage liner should be changed daily you might want to use newspaper to line the cage instead of buying cage liners – this will save you a lot of money. Another time-saving trick is to put several layers of newspaper down on the bottom of your cage. Then, when it is time for cleaning, you can just remove the top layer.

When it comes to cleaning your food and water bowls as well as your bird bath you need to clean as well as disinfect the object. Clean the dishes in hot soapy water then rinse well. To disinfect, dip the dishes in a mixture of ½ cup of bleach to 1 gallon of water. Let the dishes soak for 5 to 10 minutes then rinse well and dry completely before refilling them and putting them back in the cage. Daily cleaning and disinfecting is very important.

Weekly/Monthly Cleaning Tasks

In addition to cleaning your finch cage accessories on a daily basis you should clean the whole cage thoroughly about once a week. If you keep a single finch you might be able to wait and clean the cage only every other week or even once a month. For multiple finches, however, it is best to clean the cage weekly. To do this you will need to remove your birds to a safe place – you'll want to keep a backup cage around for this purpose.

To clean the cage, remove everything that is not permanently attached and clean the items individually using hot, soapy water. Again, disinfect everything with a bleach solution then rinse well and dry them completely. To clean the cage itself you should use a bird-friendly disinfectant spray and wipe down the entire cage. Once the accessories are cleaned, disinfected, and dried you can reassemble the cage.

3.) Quarantining/Introducing New Birds

Depending on the species you choose, you may be able to keep multiple finches together. If this is something you are considering, your best bet is to purchase them while they are still young and to raise them together. If you choose to add new birds later, however, you will need to quarantine the new bird to make sure it doesn't introduce any disease. Below you will find some tips for quarantining new birds:

- Quarantining is ALWAYS recommended for new birds – this practice should not be reserved for breeders.

- The new bird should be completely isolated during quarantine – keep it in an entirely separate room, if possible.

- Shut off air conditioning/heating to and from the quarantine room to avoid airborne contamination – you may have to draw in fresh air from the outside using a fan.

- Keep a close eye on your bird during the quarantine period to check for any signs of illness – refer to the information from the beginning of this chapter for symptoms.

- Maintain the quarantine long enough to ensure that any disease finishes its incubation period – this could take as long as six weeks.

- During the quarantine, be very careful not to share accessories or tools between the two cages – you should also be careful about changing your clothes and washing your hands.

- Only if your bird shows zero signs of disease after the six-week quarantine can it be considered safe to introduce him to your other canary.

If your new finches successfully make it through the quarantine period without incident you can take the necessary steps to introduce them into your cage. Again, this is a process that should not be rushed for the safety and wellbeing of all of your birds. You can start by placing the two cages in the same room so the birds can get used to each other from afar then slowly move the cages closer together over a period of several weeks and give the birds limited time together in a shared flight cage.

When you are ready to permanently combine the birds, make sure the cage is thoroughly cleaned and arranged so that each bird can have its own territory. Refer to the information in Chapter Five about keeping multiple finches together to determine the right size cage for keeping more than one finch.

Chapter Eight: Finch Care Sheet

Before you bring home a finch or two of your own, there is a lot to learn about the different finch species. When you are trying to decide which species is right for you, or when you are ready to start preparing your home for your new pet, you may find that you need to reference key pieces of information. Rather than flipping through the entire book to find what you need, compiled in this chapter is a list of important facts about finches divided into four categories: Basic Information, Cage Setup Guide, Nutritional Information and Breeding Tips. Simply choose the relevant category to find the facts you need to know.

1.) Basic Information

Classification: order Passeriformes; family Fringillidae, Estrildidae, Emberizidae, or Thraupidae

Distribution: primarily the Northern Hemisphere; true finches are found worldwide except in Australia and arctic regions; estrildid finches are found in Australia and in Old World tropical regions

Habitat: primarily forested areas; some species can be found in the desert or mountainous regions

Anatomical Adaptations: large, stout bills adapted to specific dietary preferences

Eggs: generally 3 to 8 per clutch; 2 to 3 broods per year; eggs are usually colored

Incubation Period: average 13 to 14 days

Hatchling: young birds leave the next after 14 to 21 days, average 15 to 17 days

Smallest Size: Andean Siskin (*Spinus spinescens*) at 3.8 inches (9.5 cm)

Largest Size: Collared Grosbeak (*Mycerobas affinis*) at 9.4 inches (24 cm)

Wingspan: about 8 to 9 inches (20 to 23 cm)

Coloration: wide variety of colors and patterns; base color is usually gray or green; many species exhibit black patches or bars; red and yellow is common

Sexual Dimorphism: male is more brightly colored and tends to sing more

Diet: mostly seeds (granivorous); some species eat berries and small insects

Vocalization: most species vocalize with males of the species singing the most; some species can be very loud and boisterous

Lifespan: average 4 to 7 years

2.) Cage Set-up Guide

Minimum Cage Dimensions: 30 by 18 by 18 inches (76x46x46 cm) for a single pair; larger for multiple pairs

Cage Shape: longer is better to accommodate natural flight pattern; flight cages are ideal

Minimum Height: 18 inches (46 cm)

Bar Spacing: no more than ½ inch, ¼ inch is better

Required Accessories: food and water dishes, perches, bathing tub, nesting box/materials, cuttlebone, toys

Food/Water Dish: at least one per pair; made from stainless steel, ceramic, or other heavy duty materials

Positioning Dishes: space them throughout the cage

Perches: at least three in different locations; stagger heights to accommodate flight; no completely smooth or sandpaper perches

Recommended Toys: rope toys, stainless steel bells, swings, etc.; keep an assortment with at least 3 toys in the cage at all times; rotate often

Bathing Tub: heavy duty materials, 1 to 2 inches water; on floor of cage or mounted to the side

Nests: nesting box made from wood or bamboo; mounted to side or back of the cage near the top

Nesting Materials: soft wood shavings, small twigs, other soft materials

Materials for Homemade Cage: plywood top and bottom, 1-by-2 inch supports, welded wire mesh enclosure

Recommended Temperature Range: warm temperatures, between 60°F and 70°F (15.5°C to 21°C), no more than 78°F (25.5°C); nighttime temperature no lower than 40°F (4.5°C)

Humidity: doesn't need to be too high, between 50% to 60% is adequate; higher humidity may be beneficial for breeding

3.) Nutritional Information

Diet in the Wild: primarily seeds, some small insects and other plant matter

Diet in Captivity: 60% to 70% seeds, 30% to 40% fresh vegetables, fruits, grains, and protein

Protein: cooked chicken egg, mealworms, other insects

Carbohydrate: whole grain bread, whole wheat bread, cooked brown rice, cooked potato, cooked sweet potato, fresh fruits and vegetables

Fats: seeds, some insects

Minerals: supplement diet with cuttlebone and/or oyster grit; powdered multivitamin optional

Supplementary Foods: fresh vegetables daily, fruit 3 times per week, cooked grains/starch and protein 2 times per week

Feeding Amount: 1 to 2 teaspoons seed daily; follow feeding recommendations on pellet package; small amounts of supplementary foods

Feeding Tips: one food dish per bird, spaced throughout the cage; shallow dishes, clean daily; offer fresh water at all times

4.) Breeding Tips

Sexual Dimorphism: males are more brightly colored (especially during breeding season) and better singers; examples include Gouldian Finch and Strawberry Finch

Sexual Monomorphism: males and females have no significant physical differences; examples include Society Finch, Spice Finch and Owl Finch

Breeding Season: usually begins in the spring in the wild; some finches breed freely in captivity

Sexual Maturity: around 6 to 9 months

Breeding Age (male): under 5 years old

Breeding Age (female): at least 1 year old

Preparing for Breeding: condition finches with high-protein diet (extra calcium for females); house male and female in separate cages next to each other for several weeks

Breeding Cage: about 18x11x14 inches (46x28x36 cm); equipped with pan of nesting materials; breeding box/nest made of wicker or wood

Recommended Nesting Materials: soft wood shavings, small twigs, other soft bedding materials

Courtship Behavior: female begins to build the nest, male starts to court the female at onset of breeding season; if female is willing, she will crouch down and allow for mating

Egg Laying: female lays one egg per day; eggs are usually colored, often with speckling

Clutch Size: 3 to 8 eggs per clutch, varies from one species to another

Incubation Period: 13 to 14 days on average

Hatching: female might take a bath and return to the nest to wet the eggs, softening them for hatching

Raising Chicks: both parents tend to care for the chicks

Fledging: chicks typically leave the nest around day 21

Breeding Frequency: average 2 to 3 clutches per year

Index

C

D

J

L

M

N

Q

R

S

T

U

V

W

Z

References

"A List of the Orders of the Class Aves: Birds." Earthlife.net. <http://www.earthlife.net/birds/orders.html>

"Bird Cage Cleaning: Daily, Weekly, and Monthly Bird Cage Maintenance." PetEducation.com. <http://www.peteducation. com/article.cfm?c=15+1794&aid=2837>

"Bird Terminology." Birds of North America. <http://www.birds-of-north-america.net/Bird_Terminology.html>

"Birds You Don't Need a License to Keep." Office of Environment and Heritage. <http://www.environment.nsw. gov.au/wildlifelicences/BirdsYouDontNeedALicenceToK eep.htm>

"Breeding Behaviors." Finch Information Center. <http://www.finchinfo.com/breeding/behaviors.php>

"Choosing a Healthy Bird." About Home. <http://birds. about.com/od/adoptingabird/a/babybirds.htm>

"Common Finch Diseases." Beauty of Birds.
<https://www.beautyofbirds.com/finchdiseases.html>

"Cost of Owning a Bird: Setup, Supplies, and Veterinary Care." PetEducation.com. <http://www.peteducation.com/article.cfm?c=15+1794&aid=1516>

"Finch Species Profiles." FinchInfo.com.
<http://www.finchinfo.com/birds/finches/species/index.php>

"Grooming Pet Birds: How to Clip Wings, Trim Beaks and Nails, and Bathe Your Bird." PetEducation.com.
<http://www.peteducation.com/article.cfm?c=15+1794&aid=180>

"How to Build a Bird Cage." Pet Care GT. <http://www.petcaregt.com/petcare/howtobuildabirdcage.html>

"Ideal Lighting, Temperature, and Humidity." Finch Information Center. <http://www.finchinfo.com/housing/lighting_temperature_humidity.php>

"Inspecting and Choosing a Healthy Bird." Psittacine Breeding & Research Farm.
<http://www.parrotpro.com/inspect.php>

Lieberman, Karl. "Try a Finch as a Pet Bird."
    BirdChannel.com. <http://www.birdchannel.com/bird-
    species/find-the-right-bird/try-a-finch.aspx>

"List of Migratory Bird Species Protected by the Migratory
    Bird Treaty Act as of December 2, 2013." U.S. Fish &
    Wildlife Service Migratory Bird Program.
    <http://www.fws.gov/migratorybirds/RegulationsPolicies
    /mbta/MBTANDX.HTML

"Nail Clipping." Finch Aviary. <http://www.finchaviary.
    com/Maintenance/NailClipping.htm>

"Permits." U.S. Fish & Wildlife Service Migratory Bird
    Program. <http://www.fws.gov/migratorybirds/
    mbpermits.html>

"Pros and Cons of Buying a Canary or Other Pet Finch."
    Students with Birds. <https://studentswithbirds.
    wordpress.com/2013/12/22/pros-and-cons-of-buying-a-
    canary-or-other-pet-finch/>

"Safe Plants and Toxic Plants." Finch Information Center.
    <http://www.finchinfo.com/housing/safe_and_toxic_plan
    ts.php>

"Species and Mutations." eFinch.com.
<http://www.efinch.com/varieties.htm>

"The Migratory Bird Treaty Act of 1918." Maryland
Department of Natural Resources.
<http://www.dnr.state.md.us/wildlife/
Plants_Wildlife/MBirdTreatyAct.asp>

"The Lady Gouldian Finch." Finch Information Center.
<http://www.finchinfo.com/birds/finches/species/lady_go
uldian_finch.php>

"The Owl (Bicheno) Finch." Finch Information Center.
<http://www.finchinfo.com/birds/finches/species/owl_fin
ch.php>

"The Red Avadavat (Strawberry Finch)." Finch Information
Center. <http://www.finchinfo.com/birds/finches/
species/red_avadavat.php>

"The Society (Bengalese Finch)." Finch Information Center.
<http://www.finchinfo.com/birds/finches/species/society_
finch.php>

"The Spice Finch (Scaly-Breasted Munia)." Finch
Information Center. <http://www.finchinfo.com/birds/
finches/species/spice_finch.php>

"The Star Finch." Finch Information Center. <http://www.finchinfo.com/birds/finches/species/star_finch.php>

"The Zebra Finch." Finch Information Center. <http://www.finchinfo.com/birds/finches/species/zebra_finch.php>

Feeding Baby
Cynthia Cherry
978-1941070000

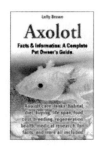

Axolotl
Lolly Brown
978-0989658430

Dysautonomia, POTS
Syndrome
Frederick Earlstein
978-0989658485

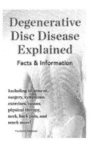

Degenerative Disc
Disease Explained
Frederick Earlstein
978-0989658485

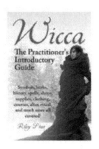

Sinusitis, Hay Fever,
Allergic Rhinitis Explained
Frederick Earlstein
978-1941070024

Wicca
Riley Star
978-1941070130

Zombie Apocalypse
Rex Cutty
978-1941070154

Capybara
Lolly Brown
978-1941070062

Eels As Pets
Lolly Brown
978-1941070167

Scabies and Lice Explained
Frederick Earlstein
978-1941070017

Saltwater Fish As Pets
Lolly Brown
978-0989658461

Torticollis Explained
Frederick Earlstein
978-1941070055

Kennel Cough
Lolly Brown
978-0989658409

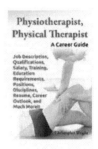

Physiotherapist, Physical
Therapist
Christopher Wright
978-0989658492

Rats, Mice, and Dormice
As Pets
Lolly Brown
978-1941070079

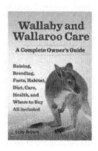

Wallaby and Wallaroo Care
Lolly Brown
978-1941070031

Bodybuilding Supplements
Explained
Jon Shelton
978-1941070239

Demonology
Riley Star
978-19401070314

Pigeon Racing
Lolly Brown
978-1941070307

Dwarf Hamster
Lolly Brown
978-1941070390

Cryptozoology
Rex Cutty
978-1941070406

Eye Strain
Frederick Earlstein
978-1941070369

Inez The Miniature Elephant
Asher Ray
978-1941070353

Vampire Apocalypse
Rex Cutty
978-1941070321

86374916R00070

Made in the USA
Lexington, KY
11 April 2018